50 Chilean Dinner Recipes for Home

By: Kelly Johnson

Table of Contents

- Pastel de Choclo
- Empanadas de Pino
- Cazuela
- Porotos Granados
- Pebre
- Charquicán
- Humitas
- Ensalada Chilena
- Pollo Arvejado
- Curanto
- Sopaipillas
- Chorrillana
- Chicha
- Pan Amasado
- Caldillo de Congrio
- Machas a la Parmesana
- Carbonada
- Sopa de Zapallo
- Completo
- Marraqueta
- Chupe de Mariscos
- Lomo a lo Pobre
- Ceviche de Reineta
- Charquican de Pavo
- Mariscal
- Mechada
- Prietas
- Mote con Huesillo
- Turrón de Vino
- Leche Asada
- Crudos
- Cola de Mono
- Pastel de Jaiba
- Pollo al Cognac
- Chapalele

- Pastel de Papas
- Berlín
- Torta de Mil Hojas
- Sopa de Cola de Mono
- Ensalada a la Chilena
- Milcaos
- Caldillo de Congrio a la Chilena
- Leche Nevada
- Pastel de Choclo a la Chilena
- Sopaipillas Pasadas
- Sopa de Cazuela
- Piure
- Machas a la Parmesana
- Pantrucas
- Sopa de Lentejas

Pastel de Choclo

Ingredients:

For the Filling:

- 1 lb ground beef or turkey
- 1 onion, finely chopped
- 2 cloves garlic, minced
- 1 red bell pepper, diced
- 1 green bell pepper, diced
- 1 tablespoon olive oil
- 1 teaspoon ground cumin
- 1 teaspoon paprika
- Salt and pepper to taste
- 1/2 cup black olives, sliced (optional)
- 1/2 cup raisins (optional)
- 2 hard-boiled eggs, sliced (optional)

For the Corn Topping (Choclo):

- 6 ears of corn, kernels removed (about 4 cups)
- 1/2 cup milk
- 2 tablespoons butter
- 1 tablespoon sugar
- Salt to taste

Instructions:

1. Prepare the Filling:
    - In a large skillet, heat the olive oil over medium heat. Add the chopped onion and cook until translucent.
    - Add the minced garlic and diced bell peppers to the skillet. Cook until the peppers are tender.
    - Add the ground beef or turkey to the skillet. Cook until browned, breaking it up with a spoon as it cooks.
    - Season the mixture with ground cumin, paprika, salt, and pepper. Stir to combine.
    - If using, add the sliced black olives and raisins to the skillet. Cook for an additional 2-3 minutes.
    - Remove the skillet from heat and set aside.

2. Prepare the Corn Topping (Choclo):
   - In a blender or food processor, blend the corn kernels with milk until smooth.
   - Transfer the blended corn mixture to a saucepan. Cook over medium heat, stirring constantly, until the mixture thickens.
   - Add the butter, sugar, and salt to the corn mixture. Stir until the butter is melted and the sugar is dissolved. Remove from heat.
3. Assemble the Pastel de Choclo:
   - Preheat the oven to 375°F (190°C).
   - Spread the meat filling evenly in the bottom of a greased baking dish.
   - Arrange the sliced hard-boiled eggs on top of the filling (if using).
   - Pour the corn mixture over the filling, spreading it out evenly to cover the filling completely.
4. Bake the Pastel de Choclo:
   - Place the baking dish in the preheated oven and bake for 30-40 minutes, or until the corn topping is golden brown and set.
5. Serve:
   - Allow the Pastel de Choclo to cool for a few minutes before serving.
   - Serve warm and enjoy this delicious Chilean comfort food!
6. Optional Garnishes:
   - Garnish with chopped fresh cilantro or parsley before serving, if desired.
7. Note:
   - Pastel de Choclo can be served as a main dish accompanied by a salad, or as a side dish with grilled meats.

Empanadas de Pino

Ingredients:

For the Dough:

- 3 cups all-purpose flour
- 1 teaspoon salt
- 1/2 cup (1 stick) unsalted butter, cold and cut into small cubes
- 1/2 cup water, cold

For the Filling (Pino):

- 1 lb ground beef
- 1 onion, finely chopped
- 2 cloves garlic, minced
- 1 tablespoon olive oil
- 1 teaspoon ground cumin
- 1 teaspoon paprika
- 1/2 teaspoon dried oregano
- Salt and pepper to taste
- 1/2 cup beef or chicken broth
- 1/2 cup black olives, sliced
- 2 hard-boiled eggs, chopped
- Raisins (optional)

For Assembly:

- 1 egg, beaten (for egg wash)

Instructions:

1. Prepare the Dough:
    - In a large mixing bowl, combine the flour and salt.
    - Add the cold cubed butter to the flour mixture. Use your fingers or a pastry cutter to cut the butter into the flour until the mixture resembles coarse crumbs.
    - Gradually add the cold water, a little at a time, mixing until the dough comes together and forms a ball. Be careful not to overwork the dough.
    - Wrap the dough in plastic wrap and refrigerate for at least 30 minutes.
2. Prepare the Filling (Pino):

- In a skillet, heat the olive oil over medium heat. Add the chopped onion and cook until translucent.
- Add the minced garlic to the skillet and cook for another minute.
- Add the ground beef to the skillet and cook until browned, breaking it up with a spoon as it cooks.
- Stir in the ground cumin, paprika, dried oregano, salt, and pepper. Cook for another minute to toast the spices.
- Pour in the beef or chicken broth and stir to combine. Simmer for about 10 minutes, or until the liquid has evaporated.
- Remove the skillet from heat and let the filling cool slightly.
- Once cooled, stir in the sliced black olives, chopped hard-boiled eggs, and raisins (if using). Set aside.

3. Assemble the Empanadas:
    - Preheat the oven to 375°F (190°C) and line a baking sheet with parchment paper.
    - On a floured surface, roll out the chilled dough to about 1/8 inch thickness. Use a round cutter (about 4-6 inches in diameter) to cut out circles of dough.
    - Place a spoonful of the filling in the center of each dough circle.
    - Fold the dough over the filling to create a half-moon shape. Use a fork to crimp the edges and seal the empanadas. Alternatively, you can twist and fold the edges to create a rope-like pattern.
    - Place the assembled empanadas on the prepared baking sheet.
4. Bake the Empanadas:
    - Brush the tops of the empanadas with beaten egg for a golden finish.
    - Bake in the preheated oven for 20-25 minutes, or until the empanadas are golden brown and crispy.
5. Serve:
    - Allow the empanadas to cool for a few minutes before serving.
    - Enjoy these delicious empanadas de pino as a snack, appetizer, or main dish, served with your favorite dipping sauce or salsa.

Cazuela

Ingredients:

- 1 lb chicken thighs, bone-in, skin-on
- 1 lb beef chuck roast, cut into chunks
- 2 tablespoons olive oil
- 1 onion, chopped
- 3 cloves garlic, minced
- 2 carrots, sliced
- 2 potatoes, peeled and diced
- 1 cup butternut squash, diced (optional)
- 1 cup green beans, trimmed and cut into bite-sized pieces
- 1 cup corn kernels
- 1 cup pumpkin, diced (optional)
- 1 red bell pepper, chopped
- 4 cups chicken or beef broth
- 1 cup tomato sauce
- 1 teaspoon ground cumin
- 1 teaspoon paprika
- 1 teaspoon dried oregano
- Salt and pepper to taste
- Fresh cilantro or parsley for garnish

Instructions:

1. Prepare the Meat:
    - Season the chicken thighs and beef chuck roast with salt and pepper.
    - In a large pot or Dutch oven, heat olive oil over medium-high heat. Brown the chicken thighs and beef chunks on all sides. Remove and set aside.
2. Sauté Aromatics:
    - In the same pot, add chopped onion and minced garlic. Sauté until translucent and fragrant.
3. Simmer with Broth:
    - Return the browned meat to the pot. Add carrots, potatoes, butternut squash, green beans, corn kernels, pumpkin, and red bell pepper.
    - Pour in chicken or beef broth and tomato sauce. Stir to combine.
4. Season and Cook:

    - Season the cazuela with ground cumin, paprika, dried oregano, salt, and pepper.
    - Bring to a boil, then reduce the heat to low. Cover and simmer for about 30-40 minutes, or until the meat is tender and the vegetables are cooked through.
5. Serve:
    - Ladle the cazuela into serving bowls. Garnish with fresh cilantro or parsley.
    - Serve hot and enjoy this hearty and comforting Chilean stew.
6. Optional:
    - You can add other vegetables like peas, zucchini, or squash according to your preference.
    - Some variations include adding rice or pasta to the cazuela for a heartier meal. Adjust the cooking time accordingly.

Porotos Granados

Ingredients:

- 2 cups fresh cranberry beans (or dried cranberry beans soaked overnight)
- 2 tablespoons olive oil
- 1 onion, chopped
- 2 cloves garlic, minced
- 2 cups corn kernels (fresh or frozen)
- 2 cups pumpkin or butternut squash, diced
- 1 cup green beans, trimmed and cut into bite-sized pieces
- 1 teaspoon ground cumin
- 1 teaspoon paprika
- 1 teaspoon dried oregano
- Salt and pepper to taste
- 4 cups vegetable or chicken broth
- 2 tablespoons fresh basil or cilantro, chopped (for garnish)

Instructions:

1. Prepare the Beans:
   - If using dried cranberry beans, soak them in water overnight. Drain and rinse before cooking.
   - In a large pot, cover the fresh or soaked dried cranberry beans with water. Bring to a boil, then reduce the heat and simmer for about 45 minutes to 1 hour, or until the beans are tender. Drain and set aside.
2. Sauté Aromatics:
   - In the same pot, heat olive oil over medium heat. Add chopped onion and minced garlic. Sauté until softened and fragrant.
3. Add Vegetables:
   - Stir in corn kernels, diced pumpkin or butternut squash, and green beans. Cook for a few minutes until the vegetables start to soften.
4. Season and Simmer:
   - Add the cooked cranberry beans to the pot.
   - Season with ground cumin, paprika, dried oregano, salt, and pepper.
   - Pour in vegetable or chicken broth. Bring to a simmer and cook for another 15-20 minutes, allowing the flavors to meld together and the vegetables to fully cook.
5. Serve:

- Ladle the porotos granados into serving bowls.
- Garnish with fresh basil or cilantro.
- Serve hot and enjoy this flavorful Chilean bean stew!
6. Optional:
    - You can add diced tomatoes or bell peppers for extra flavor and color.
    - Adjust the seasoning according to your taste preferences. You can also add a dash of hot sauce for a spicy kick.

Pebre

Ingredients:

- 2 medium tomatoes, finely diced
- 1/2 onion, finely chopped
- 1/4 cup fresh cilantro, chopped
- 1/4 cup fresh parsley, chopped
- 2 cloves garlic, minced
- 1 jalapeño pepper, seeded and finely chopped (adjust to taste)
- 2 tablespoons red wine vinegar or white vinegar
- 2 tablespoons olive oil
- Salt and pepper to taste

Instructions:

1. Combine Ingredients:
    - In a mixing bowl, combine the diced tomatoes, chopped onion, chopped cilantro, chopped parsley, minced garlic, and finely chopped jalapeño pepper.
2. Season:
    - Season the mixture with red wine vinegar or white vinegar, olive oil, salt, and pepper. Adjust the seasoning according to your taste preferences.
3. Mix Well:
    - Stir all the ingredients together until well combined. Make sure the vegetables are evenly coated with the dressing.
4. Chill:
    - Cover the bowl with plastic wrap and refrigerate the pebre for at least 30 minutes to allow the flavors to meld together and develop.
5. Serve:
    - Once chilled, give the pebre a final stir and taste. Adjust the seasoning if necessary.
    - Serve the pebre as a condiment or salsa alongside grilled meats, seafood, or with bread as an appetizer.
6. Enjoy!
Enjoy this refreshing and flavorful Chilean salsa with your favorite dishes or as a dip for tortilla chips!

Charquicán

Ingredients:

- 1 lb beef jerky (charqui), chopped into small pieces
- 2 tablespoons vegetable oil
- 1 onion, finely chopped
- 2 cloves garlic, minced
- 2 carrots, peeled and diced
- 2 potatoes, peeled and diced
- 1 cup pumpkin or butternut squash, diced
- 1 cup green beans, trimmed and cut into bite-sized pieces
- 1 cup corn kernels
- 1/2 cup peas (fresh or frozen)
- 2 tomatoes, diced
- 2 cups beef or vegetable broth
- Salt and pepper to taste
- Fresh cilantro or parsley for garnish

Instructions:

1. Prepare the Beef Jerky:
    - If the beef jerky is very salty, soak it in water for about 1 hour to remove excess salt. Drain and chop into small pieces.
2. Sauté Aromatics:
    - In a large pot or Dutch oven, heat vegetable oil over medium heat. Add chopped onion and minced garlic. Sauté until softened and fragrant.
3. Add Vegetables:
    - Add diced carrots, potatoes, pumpkin or butternut squash, green beans, corn kernels, peas, and diced tomatoes to the pot. Stir to combine.
4. Cook with Broth:
    - Pour in beef or vegetable broth. Bring to a simmer and cook for about 20-25 minutes, or until the vegetables are tender.
5. Add Beef Jerky:
    - Add the chopped beef jerky to the pot. Stir to combine with the vegetables and broth.
6. Season:
    - Season the charquicán with salt and pepper to taste. Adjust the seasoning according to your preference.

7. Simmer:
    - Continue to simmer the charquicán for another 5-10 minutes, allowing the flavors to meld together.
8. Serve:
    - Ladle the charquicán into serving bowls. Garnish with fresh cilantro or parsley.
9. Enjoy!
   Serve hot and enjoy this hearty and comforting Chilean stew! It's perfect for a cozy dinner on a cold day.

Humitas

Ingredients:

- 6 large ears of fresh corn, husks and silk removed
- 1/2 cup unsalted butter, softened
- 1/2 cup milk
- 1/2 cup cornmeal
- 1/4 cup granulated sugar (optional)
- Salt to taste
- Banana leaves or corn husks, for wrapping (optional)

Instructions:

1. Prepare the Corn:
    - Grate the kernels off the corn cobs using a box grater or cut them off with a knife. Reserve the corn kernels and discard the cobs.
2. Make the Humita Mixture:
    - In a large mixing bowl, combine the grated corn, softened butter, milk, cornmeal, and granulated sugar (if using). Mix well until all ingredients are fully incorporated.
    - Season the mixture with salt to taste. Adjust the sweetness by adding more sugar if desired.
3. Prepare the Wrappers:
    - If using banana leaves, cut them into squares of about 8x8 inches. If using corn husks, soak them in warm water for about 30 minutes to soften.
4. Assemble the Humitas:
    - Place about 2 tablespoons of the humita mixture onto the center of each banana leaf or corn husk.
    - Fold the sides of the wrapper over the mixture to enclose it, then fold the top and bottom edges to form a neat package. Tie the humitas securely with kitchen twine if necessary.
5. Steam the Humitas:
    - Arrange the wrapped humitas in a steamer basket, making sure they are not overcrowded.
    - Steam the humitas over simmering water for about 45-60 minutes, or until the mixture is firm and cooked through. The cooking time may vary depending on the size of the humitas.
6. Serve:

- Once cooked, carefully unwrap the humitas and serve them hot.
- Enjoy these delicious and comforting Chilean corn cakes as a snack, side dish, or light meal.

7. Optional:
    - You can add other ingredients to the humita mixture such as cheese, diced peppers, or cooked onions for extra flavor and texture.
    - Traditionally, humitas are served with aji sauce or pebre, a Chilean salsa, on the side for dipping.

Ensalada Chilena

Ingredients:

- 4 large tomatoes, sliced
- 1 large onion, thinly sliced into rings
- 1 bunch fresh cilantro, chopped
- 2 tablespoons red wine vinegar or white vinegar
- 2 tablespoons olive oil
- Salt and pepper to taste

Instructions:

1. Prepare the Vegetables:
    - Wash the tomatoes and slice them into rounds.
    - Peel the onion and thinly slice it into rings.
    - Chop the fresh cilantro.
2. Assemble the Salad:
    - Arrange the tomato slices on a serving platter.
    - Top the tomatoes with the sliced onion rings.
    - Sprinkle the chopped cilantro over the tomatoes and onions.
3. Prepare the Dressing:
    - In a small bowl, whisk together the red wine vinegar or white vinegar with the olive oil.
    - Season the dressing with salt and pepper to taste.
4. Dress the Salad:
    - Drizzle the dressing over the assembled salad just before serving.
    - Toss gently to coat the vegetables evenly with the dressing.
5. Serve:
    - Serve the ensalada Chilena as a refreshing side dish or appetizer.
    - Enjoy the vibrant flavors of fresh tomatoes, onions, and cilantro dressed with a simple vinaigrette.
6. Optional:
    - For added flavor, you can add diced avocado or fresh chili peppers to the salad.
    - Some variations include adding diced bell peppers or cucumber for extra crunch and color.
    - Serve the salad chilled or at room temperature, according to your preference.

Pollo Arvejado

Ingredients:

- 4 chicken thighs (bone-in and skin-on)
- Salt and pepper to taste
- 2 tablespoons olive oil
- 1 onion, finely chopped
- 2 cloves garlic, minced
- 2 carrots, peeled and sliced
- 1 cup frozen peas
- 2 tomatoes, diced
- 1 cup chicken broth
- 1/2 cup white wine (optional)
- 1 teaspoon paprika
- 1 teaspoon ground cumin
- 1/2 teaspoon dried oregano
- Fresh parsley, chopped, for garnish

Instructions:

1. Season and Brown the Chicken:
    - Season the chicken thighs with salt and pepper.
    - In a large skillet or Dutch oven, heat the olive oil over medium-high heat. Add the chicken thighs, skin side down, and cook until golden brown on both sides. Remove the chicken from the skillet and set aside.
2. Sauté Aromatics:
    - In the same skillet, add the chopped onion and minced garlic. Sauté until softened and fragrant.
3. Add Vegetables:
    - Add the sliced carrots to the skillet and cook for a few minutes until they begin to soften.
    - Stir in the frozen peas and diced tomatoes. Cook for another minute.
4. Deglaze and Simmer:
    - Pour in the chicken broth and white wine (if using), scraping up any browned bits from the bottom of the skillet.
    - Return the chicken thighs to the skillet. Sprinkle the paprika, ground cumin, and dried oregano over the chicken and vegetables.
5. Simmer:

- - Reduce the heat to low, cover the skillet, and simmer for about 20-25 minutes, or until the chicken is cooked through and the vegetables are tender.
6. Serve:
    - Transfer the chicken thighs and vegetables to a serving platter.
    - Garnish with chopped fresh parsley.
    - Serve the pollo arvejado hot, accompanied by rice, potatoes, or crusty bread.
7. Enjoy!
   Enjoy this comforting and flavorful Chilean chicken stew with your favorite sides for a delicious meal!

Curanto

Ingredients:

For the Earth Oven:

- Large pit or hole in the ground
- Rocks

For the Curanto:

- 1 lb beef, cut into chunks
- 1 lb pork, cut into chunks
- 1 lb chicken, cut into pieces
- 1 lb chorizo sausages
- 1 lb lamb, cut into chunks (optional)
- 2 lb fresh seafood (such as clams, mussels, shrimp, and fish fillets)
- 2 lb potatoes, peeled and halved
- 2 lb sweet potatoes, peeled and halved
- 2 lb butternut squash, peeled and cut into chunks
- 2 lb fresh corn on the cob, husks removed and halved
- 1 bunch fresh cilantro, chopped
- 1 bunch fresh parsley, chopped
- Salt and pepper to taste
- Banana leaves or aluminum foil

Instructions:

1. Prepare the Earth Oven:
    - Dig a large pit or hole in the ground and line it with rocks. Build a fire in the pit and let it burn until the rocks are hot.
2. Layer the Ingredients:
    - Season the beef, pork, chicken, lamb (if using), and chorizo sausages with salt and pepper.
    - Layer the seasoned meats, seafood, potatoes, sweet potatoes, butternut squash, and corn on the cob in the pit, alternating between layers of meat and vegetables.
    - Sprinkle chopped cilantro and parsley over each layer.
3. Cover and Cook:
    - Cover the ingredients with banana leaves or aluminum foil to create a seal.

        - Cover the pit with more rocks and dirt to trap the heat inside.
        - Let the curanto cook in the earth oven for about 1-2 hours, depending on the size of the pit and the amount of food.
4. Serve:
        - Carefully uncover the curanto and remove the cooked ingredients from the pit.
        - Serve the curanto hot, family-style, on large platters or banana leaves.
        - Enjoy the delicious flavors of the mixed seafood, meats, and vegetables cooked together in the earth oven!
5. Note:
        - Traditional curanto recipes may vary depending on the region and availability of ingredients. Feel free to customize the recipe with your favorite meats, seafood, and vegetables.

Sopaipillas

Ingredients:

- 2 cups all-purpose flour
- 1 cup cooked, mashed pumpkin (canned pumpkin puree can also be used)
- 1 teaspoon baking powder
- 1/2 teaspoon salt
- 1/2 teaspoon ground cinnamon (optional)
- 1/4 teaspoon ground nutmeg (optional)
- Vegetable oil, for frying
- Honey or pebre (Chilean salsa), for serving

Instructions:

1. Prepare the Dough:
    - In a large mixing bowl, combine the all-purpose flour, mashed pumpkin, baking powder, salt, ground cinnamon, and ground nutmeg (if using).
    - Mix the ingredients together until a soft dough forms. Add a little more flour if the dough is too sticky, or a little more pumpkin if it's too dry.
2. Roll Out the Dough:
    - On a lightly floured surface, roll out the dough to about 1/4 inch thickness.
3. Cut Into Shapes:
    - Use a knife or pastry cutter to cut the dough into small circles, squares, or triangles, depending on your preference. You can also use a round cookie cutter or the rim of a drinking glass.
4. Fry the Sopaipillas:
    - In a large skillet or deep fryer, heat vegetable oil to 350°F (175°C).
    - Carefully add the sopaipillas to the hot oil, a few at a time, making sure not to overcrowd the pan.
    - Fry the sopaipillas for 2-3 minutes on each side, or until golden brown and puffed up.
5. Drain and Serve:
    - Use a slotted spoon to transfer the fried sopaipillas to a plate lined with paper towels to drain any excess oil.
    - Serve the sopaipillas hot with a drizzle of honey or alongside pebre, a Chilean salsa, for dipping.

6. Enjoy!
   Enjoy these delicious and comforting Chilean pastries as a snack, dessert, or appetizer! They're best served hot and fresh from the fryer.

Chorrillana

Ingredients:

- 1 lb beef sirloin or skirt steak, thinly sliced
- 4 large potatoes, peeled and cut into french fries
- 2 large onions, thinly sliced
- 4 eggs
- 4 cloves garlic, minced
- 1/4 cup vegetable oil
- Salt and pepper to taste
- Fresh parsley, chopped, for garnish

Instructions:

1. Prepare the French Fries:
   - Heat vegetable oil in a deep fryer or large skillet over medium-high heat.
   - Fry the potato slices in batches until golden brown and crispy. Remove from the oil and drain on paper towels. Season with salt and set aside.
2. Cook the Beef:
   - In the same skillet or another large skillet, heat a little more vegetable oil over medium-high heat.
   - Add the thinly sliced beef to the skillet and cook until browned and cooked through, about 3-4 minutes per side. Season with salt and pepper to taste. Remove from the skillet and set aside.
3. Sauté the Onions and Garlic:
   - In the same skillet, add the sliced onions and minced garlic. Sauté until the onions are soft and caramelized, about 8-10 minutes.
4. Assemble the Chorrillana:
   - Return the cooked beef to the skillet with the onions and garlic.
   - Add the cooked french fries to the skillet, arranging them in an even layer on top of the beef and onions.
5. Fry the Eggs:
   - In a separate skillet, fry the eggs to your desired doneness (usually sunny-side up or over easy).
6. Serve:
   - Transfer the chorrillana to a large serving platter or individual plates.
   - Top with the fried eggs and sprinkle with chopped fresh parsley.

7. Enjoy!
   Serve the chorrillana hot and enjoy this delicious and satisfying Chilean dish with your favorite condiments, such as ketchup, mayonnaise, or hot sauce. It's perfect for sharing with friends and family!

Chicha

Ingredients:

- 2 lbs dried maize (corn)
- 1 cinnamon stick
- 3 cloves
- 1/2 cup brown sugar or piloncillo (traditional raw sugar)
- Water
- Optional: additional spices such as anise, allspice, or ginger for flavor variation

Instructions:

1. Prepare the Maize:
    - Rinse the dried maize thoroughly under cold water to remove any dirt or debris.
2. Soak the Maize:
    - Place the dried maize in a large bowl or pot and cover with water. Allow the maize to soak overnight or for at least 8 hours to soften.
3. Boil the Maize:
    - Drain the soaked maize and transfer it to a large pot. Add enough water to cover the maize by a few inches.
    - Add the cinnamon stick and cloves to the pot.
    - Bring the water to a boil over medium-high heat, then reduce the heat to low and simmer for 1-2 hours, or until the maize is tender. Skim off any foam that rises to the surface during cooking.
4. Sweeten the Chicha:
    - Once the maize is cooked, remove the pot from the heat and let it cool slightly.
    - Stir in the brown sugar or piloncillo until dissolved. Adjust the sweetness to taste.
5. Fermentation:
    - Transfer the cooked maize and liquid (now called "chicha") to a large glass or ceramic container.
    - Cover the container loosely with a clean cloth or plastic wrap, allowing air to circulate.
    - Place the container in a cool, dark place and let the chicha ferment for 1-3 days, depending on the desired level of fermentation. Stir the chicha occasionally during fermentation.

6. Strain and Serve:
   - After fermentation, strain the chicha through a fine mesh sieve or cheesecloth to remove the solids.
   - Transfer the strained chicha to clean bottles or jars and refrigerate until cold.
7. Enjoy!
   Serve the chilled chicha in glasses with ice cubes, if desired. Garnish with a sprinkle of ground cinnamon or a cinnamon stick for added flavor. Enjoy this traditional Chilean drink as a refreshing beverage on a hot day or as a special treat for celebrations and gatherings.

Pan Amasado

Ingredients:

- 4 cups all-purpose flour
- 1 teaspoon salt
- 1 tablespoon granulated sugar
- 1 tablespoon active dry yeast
- 1 1/4 cups warm water
- 1/4 cup vegetable oil or melted butter
- Optional: additional flour for dusting

Instructions:

1. Activate the Yeast:
   - In a small bowl, dissolve the granulated sugar in the warm water. Sprinkle the active dry yeast over the water and let it sit for about 5-10 minutes, or until the mixture becomes frothy.
2. Prepare the Dough:
   - In a large mixing bowl, combine the all-purpose flour and salt. Make a well in the center of the flour mixture.
   - Pour the activated yeast mixture and vegetable oil or melted butter into the well.
3. Knead the Dough:
   - Using a wooden spoon or your hands, gradually incorporate the flour into the wet ingredients until a rough dough forms.
   - Turn the dough out onto a floured surface and knead it for about 8-10 minutes, or until it becomes smooth, elastic, and no longer sticky. Add more flour as needed to prevent sticking, but be careful not to add too much, as it can make the bread dense.
4. First Rise:
   - Place the kneaded dough in a greased bowl and cover it with a clean kitchen towel or plastic wrap.
   - Let the dough rise in a warm, draft-free place for about 1-2 hours, or until it has doubled in size.
5. Shape the Bread:
   - Punch down the risen dough to release the air bubbles.
   - Divide the dough into equal-sized portions and shape each portion into a round ball or oval shape.

6. Second Rise:
   - Place the shaped dough balls onto a baking sheet lined with parchment paper, leaving some space between each one.
   - Cover the dough balls with a clean kitchen towel or plastic wrap and let them rise for another 30-45 minutes, or until they have doubled in size.
7. Bake the Bread:
   - Preheat your oven to 375°F (190°C).
   - Once the dough balls have risen, bake them in the preheated oven for 20-25 minutes, or until they are golden brown on top and sound hollow when tapped on the bottom.
8. Cool and Serve:
   - Transfer the baked Pan Amasado to a wire rack to cool completely before serving.
   - Enjoy the warm, fluffy bread with butter, jam, or your favorite toppings.
9. Optional:
   - For a shiny finish, brush the tops of the bread with melted butter immediately after removing them from the oven.
   - You can also sprinkle sesame seeds, poppy seeds, or coarse salt on top of the bread before baking for added flavor and texture.

Caldillo de Congrio

Ingredients:

- 2 lbs congrio fillets (substitute with cod, hake, or other firm white fish if congrio is not available)
- 1 onion, chopped
- 2 cloves garlic, minced
- 2 carrots, peeled and sliced
- 2 potatoes, peeled and diced
- 1 bell pepper, chopped
- 1 cup chopped tomatoes (fresh or canned)
- 4 cups fish or vegetable broth
- 1 cup white wine
- 2 bay leaves
- 1 teaspoon paprika
- 1/2 teaspoon ground cumin
- Salt and pepper to taste
- Olive oil for sautéing
- Fresh parsley or cilantro for garnish

Instructions:

1. Prepare the Congrio:
    - If using fresh congrio, clean and fillet the fish, removing any bones and skin. Cut the fillets into large chunks. If using frozen congrio or another type of fish, thaw it thoroughly before use.
2. Sauté Aromatics:
    - In a large pot or Dutch oven, heat some olive oil over medium heat. Add the chopped onion and minced garlic, and sauté until softened and fragrant.
3. Add Vegetables and Spices:
    - Add the sliced carrots, diced potatoes, chopped bell pepper, and chopped tomatoes to the pot. Stir in the paprika and ground cumin, and season with salt and pepper to taste.
4. Cook the Broth:
    - Pour in the fish or vegetable broth and white wine. Add the bay leaves to the pot. Bring the mixture to a simmer and cook for about 15-20 minutes, or until the vegetables are tender.

5. Add the Fish:
   - Carefully add the congrio fillets to the pot, making sure they are submerged in the broth. Simmer gently for another 5-7 minutes, or until the fish is cooked through and flakes easily with a fork.
6. Serve:
   - Ladle the caldillo de congrio into serving bowls, making sure to distribute the fish and vegetables evenly.
   - Garnish with fresh parsley or cilantro before serving.
7. Enjoy!
Serve the caldillo de congrio hot, accompanied by crusty bread or rice. It's a comforting and flavorful Chilean stew that's perfect for chilly days or anytime you crave a hearty meal.

Machas a la Parmesana

Ingredients:

- 12 fresh razor clams (machas)
- 1/2 cup butter, softened
- 2 cloves garlic, minced
- 1/2 cup breadcrumbs
- 1/2 cup grated Parmesan cheese
- 1/4 cup fresh parsley, chopped
- Salt and pepper to taste
- Lemon wedges for serving

Instructions:

1. Prepare the Razor Clams:
    - Rinse the razor clams thoroughly under cold water to remove any sand or grit. Use a small brush to scrub the shells clean.
    - Open the razor clams by inserting a knife between the shells and cutting the muscle that holds them together. Remove the clam meat from the shells and set aside.
2. Prepare the Topping:
    - In a mixing bowl, combine the softened butter, minced garlic, breadcrumbs, grated Parmesan cheese, and chopped parsley. Season with salt and pepper to taste. Mix until well combined.
3. Assemble the Dish:
    - Preheat your oven to 375°F (190°C).
    - Arrange the opened razor clam shells on a baking sheet lined with aluminum foil or parchment paper.
    - Place a portion of the razor clam meat on each shell, then top with the prepared Parmesan cheese mixture, spreading it evenly over the clam meat.
4. Bake the Machas:
    - Place the baking sheet in the preheated oven and bake the machas for 8-10 minutes, or until the topping is golden brown and bubbly.
5. Serve:
    - Remove the machas from the oven and let them cool slightly.
    - Serve the machas a la Parmesana hot, garnished with fresh parsley and lemon wedges on the side.

6. Enjoy!
   These razor clams baked with Parmesan cheese make for a delightful appetizer or seafood dish. Enjoy the rich flavors and tender texture of this classic Chilean recipe!

Carbonada

Ingredients:

- 1 lb beef chuck or stewing beef, cut into cubes
- 2 tablespoons vegetable oil
- 1 onion, chopped
- 2 cloves garlic, minced
- 2 carrots, peeled and diced
- 2 potatoes, peeled and diced
- 1 cup butternut squash or pumpkin, peeled and diced
- 1 cup corn kernels (fresh or frozen)
- 1 cup green beans, trimmed and cut into bite-sized pieces
- 1 cup peas (fresh or frozen)
- 2 tomatoes, diced
- 4 cups beef or vegetable broth
- 1/2 cup white wine (optional)
- 1/4 cup uncooked rice
- 1 teaspoon paprika
- 1/2 teaspoon ground cumin
- Salt and pepper to taste
- Fresh parsley or cilantro for garnish

Instructions:

1. Brown the Beef:
    - Heat the vegetable oil in a large pot or Dutch oven over medium-high heat. Add the beef cubes and brown them on all sides. Remove the beef from the pot and set it aside.
2. Sauté Aromatics:
    - In the same pot, add the chopped onion and minced garlic. Sauté until softened and fragrant.
3. Add Vegetables:
    - Add the diced carrots, potatoes, butternut squash or pumpkin, corn kernels, green beans, peas, and diced tomatoes to the pot. Stir to combine.
4. Cook the Stew:
    - Return the browned beef to the pot. Pour in the beef or vegetable broth and white wine (if using).

        - Add the uncooked rice, paprika, and ground cumin to the pot. Season with salt and pepper to taste.
5. Simmer:
    - Bring the stew to a simmer, then reduce the heat to low. Cover and cook for about 30-40 minutes, or until the vegetables are tender and the flavors have melded together.
6. Serve:
    - Ladle the carbonada into serving bowls. Garnish with fresh parsley or cilantro.
7. Enjoy!

Serve the carbonada hot and enjoy this delicious and comforting Chilean stew on a cold day. It pairs well with crusty bread or rice for a satisfying meal.

Sopa de Zapallo

Ingredients:

- 2 lbs butternut squash or pumpkin, peeled, seeded, and diced
- 1 onion, chopped
- 2 cloves garlic, minced
- 2 carrots, peeled and chopped
- 2 potatoes, peeled and chopped
- 4 cups vegetable or chicken broth
- 1 cup milk or cream
- 2 tablespoons olive oil or butter
- 1 teaspoon ground cumin
- 1/2 teaspoon ground nutmeg
- Salt and pepper to taste
- Fresh parsley or cilantro for garnish (optional)

Instructions:

1. Prepare the Vegetables:
    - Peel, seed, and dice the butternut squash or pumpkin. Chop the onion, garlic, carrots, and potatoes.
2. Sauté Aromatics:
    - In a large pot or Dutch oven, heat the olive oil or butter over medium heat. Add the chopped onion and garlic, and sauté until softened and fragrant.
3. Add Vegetables and Spices:
    - Add the diced butternut squash or pumpkin, chopped carrots, and potatoes to the pot. Sprinkle with ground cumin and ground nutmeg. Season with salt and pepper to taste.
4. Cook the Soup:
    - Pour in the vegetable or chicken broth, ensuring that the vegetables are submerged. Bring the mixture to a boil, then reduce the heat to low. Cover and simmer for about 20-25 minutes, or until the vegetables are tender.
5. Blend the Soup:
    - Once the vegetables are cooked, use an immersion blender to puree the soup until smooth and creamy. Alternatively, transfer the soup in batches to a blender and blend until smooth. Be careful when blending hot liquids.
6. Add Milk or Cream:

- Stir in the milk or cream, adjusting the amount to achieve your desired consistency. Heat the soup gently until warmed through.
7. Serve:
    - Ladle the sopa de zapallo into serving bowls. Garnish with fresh parsley or cilantro, if desired.
8. Enjoy!
   Serve the sopa de zapallo hot, accompanied by crusty bread or croutons for a delicious and comforting meal. It's perfect for lunch or dinner on a chilly day!

Completo

Ingredients:

- 4 hot dog buns
- 4 beef or pork hot dogs
- 1/2 cup sauerkraut
- 1/2 cup chopped tomatoes
- 1/4 cup chopped onions
- 1/4 cup chopped avocado
- 1/4 cup mayonnaise
- 1/4 cup ketchup
- 1/4 cup mustard
- 1/4 cup chopped fresh cilantro (optional)
- 1/4 cup chopped pickles (optional)
- 1/4 cup chopped jalapeños (optional)
- Salt and pepper to taste

Instructions:

1. Prepare the Hot Dogs:
    - Grill or boil the hot dogs according to your preference until cooked through.
2. Warm the Buns:
    - Lightly toast the hot dog buns on a grill or in a toaster oven until warm and slightly crispy.
3. Assemble the Completo:
    - Place a cooked hot dog in each bun.
    - Top each hot dog with sauerkraut, chopped tomatoes, chopped onions, and chopped avocado.
4. Add Condiments:
    - Drizzle mayonnaise, ketchup, and mustard over the toppings.
    - Add any additional optional toppings such as chopped cilantro, pickles, or jalapeños according to your taste.
5. Season:
    - Season the completos with salt and pepper to taste.
6. Serve:
    - Serve the completos immediately while they're still warm and the toppings are fresh.

7. Enjoy!
   Enjoy these loaded completos as a satisfying and flavorful meal. They're perfect for lunch, dinner, or as a late-night snack. Serve with your favorite side dishes or enjoy them on their own for an authentic Chilean street food experience!

Marraqueta

Ingredients:

- 4 cups all-purpose flour
- 2 teaspoons salt
- 2 teaspoons active dry yeast
- 1 1/2 cups warm water
- 1 tablespoon sugar
- Vegetable oil or cooking spray, for greasing

Instructions:

1. Activate the Yeast:
   - In a small bowl, combine the warm water, sugar, and active dry yeast. Stir gently and let it sit for about 5-10 minutes, or until the mixture becomes frothy.
2. Mix the Dough:
   - In a large mixing bowl, combine the flour and salt. Make a well in the center of the flour mixture and pour in the activated yeast mixture.
   - Using a wooden spoon or your hands, mix the ingredients until a rough dough forms.
3. Knead the Dough:
   - Transfer the dough to a lightly floured surface and knead it for about 8-10 minutes, or until it becomes smooth and elastic. Add more flour if the dough is too sticky.
4. First Rise:
   - Place the kneaded dough in a greased bowl, turning it to coat with oil. Cover the bowl with a clean kitchen towel or plastic wrap and let the dough rise in a warm, draft-free place for about 1-2 hours, or until it doubles in size.
5. Shape the Loaves:
   - Once the dough has risen, punch it down to release the air bubbles. Divide the dough into equal-sized portions, depending on the size of marraqueta you desire.
   - Shape each portion into a round or oval loaf, then flatten slightly with your hands.
6. Second Rise:

- Place the shaped loaves on a lightly greased baking sheet, leaving some space between them. Cover the baking sheet with a clean kitchen towel or plastic wrap and let the loaves rise for another 30-45 minutes, or until they have doubled in size.
7. Preheat the Oven:
   - While the loaves are rising, preheat your oven to 425°F (220°C).
8. Score the Loaves:
   - Using a sharp knife or razor blade, make diagonal slashes on the top of each loaf to create a crosshatch pattern.
9. Bake the Marraqueta:
   - Place the baking sheet in the preheated oven and bake the marraqueta for 20-25 minutes, or until the loaves are golden brown and sound hollow when tapped on the bottom.
10. Cool and Serve:
    - Transfer the baked marraqueta to a wire rack to cool completely before slicing and serving.
11. Enjoy!

Enjoy your homemade marraqueta as a delicious addition to breakfast, lunch, or dinner. It's perfect for sandwiches, toast, or simply enjoyed on its own with butter or jam.

Chupe de Mariscos

Ingredients:

- 1 lb mixed seafood (shrimp, clams, mussels, squid, etc.), cleaned and deveined
- 1 onion, chopped
- 2 cloves garlic, minced
- 1 red bell pepper, chopped
- 1 green bell pepper, chopped
- 2 tomatoes, diced
- 2 cups fish or seafood broth
- 1 cup milk or heavy cream
- 1/4 cup white wine (optional)
- 2 tablespoons olive oil
- 2 tablespoons all-purpose flour
- 2 tablespoons chopped fresh parsley
- 1 teaspoon paprika
- 1/2 teaspoon ground cumin
- Salt and pepper to taste
- Crusty bread for serving

Instructions:

1. Prepare the Seafood:
    - Clean and devein the seafood as needed. Cut any larger seafood into bite-sized pieces.
2. Sauté Aromatics:
    - In a large pot or Dutch oven, heat the olive oil over medium heat. Add the chopped onion and minced garlic, and sauté until softened and fragrant.
3. Add Vegetables:
    - Add the chopped red bell pepper and green bell pepper to the pot. Sauté for a few minutes until the peppers are slightly softened.
4. Make the Roux:
    - Sprinkle the flour over the sautéed vegetables and stir to coat evenly. Cook for 1-2 minutes to remove the raw flour taste.
5. Add Broth and Wine:
    - Gradually pour in the fish or seafood broth, stirring constantly to avoid lumps. Add the white wine, if using, and stir to combine.
6. Season and Simmer:

- Stir in the diced tomatoes, paprika, ground cumin, salt, and pepper. Bring the mixture to a simmer and cook for about 10-15 minutes, or until the vegetables are tender and the flavors have melded together.
7. Add Milk or Cream:
    - Pour in the milk or heavy cream and stir to combine. Adjust the seasoning if necessary.
8. Add Seafood:
    - Carefully add the mixed seafood to the pot, making sure it's submerged in the broth. Cook for another 5-7 minutes, or until the seafood is cooked through.
9. Garnish and Serve:
    - Stir in the chopped fresh parsley just before serving.
    - Serve the chupe de mariscos hot, accompanied by crusty bread for dipping.
10. Enjoy!

Enjoy this delicious and comforting chupe de mariscos as a satisfying meal on its own or as part of a larger spread. It's perfect for sharing with family and friends!

Lomo a lo Pobre

Ingredients:

- 4 beef tenderloin steaks (about 6-8 oz each)
- 4 large potatoes, peeled and cut into thick fries
- 2 large onions, thinly sliced
- 4 eggs
- Vegetable oil for frying
- Salt and pepper to taste
- 1 tablespoon butter (optional, for caramelizing onions)
- 1 tablespoon sugar (optional, for caramelizing onions)
- 1 tablespoon soy sauce (optional, for marinating steak)

Instructions:

1. Marinate the Steak (optional):
    - If desired, marinate the beef tenderloin steaks in soy sauce for about 30 minutes to 1 hour before cooking. This step is optional but adds flavor to the steak.
2. Fry the Potatoes:
    - Heat vegetable oil in a deep fryer or large skillet over medium-high heat. Fry the potato fries until golden brown and crispy. Remove from the oil and drain on paper towels. Season with salt and set aside.
3. Cook the Steak:
    - Season the beef tenderloin steaks with salt and pepper on both sides. Heat a skillet or grill pan over medium-high heat and cook the steaks to your desired doneness (usually about 3-4 minutes per side for medium-rare). Once cooked, transfer the steaks to a plate and let them rest.
4. Caramelize the Onions (optional):
    - In the same skillet used to cook the steaks, melt the butter over medium heat. Add the thinly sliced onions and cook, stirring occasionally, until they become soft and golden brown. Sprinkle sugar over the onions to help caramelize them further, if desired.
5. Fry the Eggs:
    - In a separate skillet, fry the eggs to your desired doneness (usually sunny-side up or over easy).
6. Assemble the Dish:

        - Place a portion of the cooked steak on each serving plate.
        - Arrange a generous portion of fried potatoes next to the steak.
        - Top the steak with caramelized onions.
        - Place a fried egg on top of each steak.
7. Serve:
        - Serve the lomo a lo pobre hot, garnished with additional salt and pepper if desired.
8. Enjoy!
Enjoy this delicious and hearty Chilean dish with a combination of flavors and textures that will satisfy your taste buds. It's perfect for a special dinner or anytime you're craving a comforting meal.

Ceviche de Reineta

Ingredients:

- 1 lb reineta fish fillets, skinless and boneless, cut into bite-sized pieces
- 4-5 limes, juiced
- 1 lemon, juiced
- 1 red onion, thinly sliced
- 1-2 chili peppers (such as jalapeño or serrano), seeded and finely chopped
- 1/2 cup chopped fresh cilantro
- 1 garlic clove, minced
- Salt and pepper to taste
- 1 tablespoon olive oil (optional)
- 1/2 cup diced tomatoes (optional, for garnish)
- Lettuce leaves, for serving
- Corn or plantain chips, for serving

Instructions:

1. Prepare the Fish:
    - Cut the reineta fish fillets into bite-sized pieces and place them in a shallow dish or bowl.
2. Marinate the Fish:
    - Pour the lime juice and lemon juice over the fish, making sure it's fully submerged. The citrus juices will "cook" the fish, turning it opaque.
    - Cover the dish with plastic wrap and refrigerate for about 30 minutes to 1 hour, stirring occasionally to ensure all the fish is evenly marinated.
3. Prepare the Ingredients:
    - In the meantime, thinly slice the red onion, finely chop the chili peppers, and mince the garlic. Chop the fresh cilantro. If using diced tomatoes for garnish, prepare them as well.
4. Assemble the Ceviche:
    - Once the fish is "cooked" in the citrus juices, drain off most of the excess liquid.
    - Add the sliced red onion, chopped chili peppers, minced garlic, and chopped cilantro to the marinated fish. Season with salt and pepper to taste.
    - If desired, drizzle olive oil over the ceviche for added richness and flavor. Gently toss to combine all the ingredients.

5. Chill:
    - Cover the ceviche with plastic wrap and return it to the refrigerator to chill for another 15-30 minutes, allowing the flavors to meld.
6. Serve:
    - To serve, line a serving platter or individual plates with lettuce leaves.
    - Spoon the ceviche onto the lettuce leaves, garnish with diced tomatoes if using, and serve with corn or plantain chips on the side.
7. Enjoy!
Enjoy this delicious and refreshing Ceviche de Reineta as an appetizer or light meal. The bright citrus flavors combined with the freshness of the fish and aromatic herbs make it a delightful dish, perfect for warm weather or any time you're craving a taste of Chilean cuisine.

Charquican de Pavo

Ingredients:

- 2 cups shredded cooked turkey or chicken
- 2 tablespoons vegetable oil
- 1 onion, finely chopped
- 2 cloves garlic, minced
- 2 carrots, peeled and diced
- 2 potatoes, peeled and diced
- 1 cup diced pumpkin or butternut squash
- 1 cup corn kernels (fresh or frozen)
- 1 cup green peas (fresh or frozen)
- 2 cups vegetable or chicken broth
- 1 teaspoon ground cumin
- 1 teaspoon paprika
- Salt and pepper to taste
- Fresh cilantro or parsley, chopped (for garnish)

Instructions:

1. Sauté Aromatics:
    - Heat the vegetable oil in a large pot or Dutch oven over medium heat. Add the chopped onion and minced garlic, and sauté until softened and fragrant.
2. Add Vegetables:
    - Add the diced carrots, potatoes, pumpkin, corn kernels, and green peas to the pot. Stir to combine with the onions and garlic.
3. Cook Vegetables:
    - Pour in the vegetable or chicken broth, ensuring that the vegetables are submerged. Bring the mixture to a simmer and cook for about 15-20 minutes, or until the vegetables are tender.
4. Season:
    - Add the shredded cooked turkey or chicken to the pot, along with the ground cumin, paprika, salt, and pepper. Stir well to combine and allow the flavors to meld together.
5. Simmer:
    - Continue to simmer the charquicán for another 5-10 minutes, allowing the turkey or chicken to heat through and the flavors to develop.

6. Adjust Seasoning:
   - Taste the charquicán and adjust the seasoning with more salt and pepper if needed.
7. Serve:
   - Ladle the charquicán into serving bowls and garnish with chopped fresh cilantro or parsley.
8. Enjoy!
   Serve the charquicán de pavo hot, accompanied by rice or bread, if desired. It's a hearty and comforting dish that's perfect for chilly days or anytime you're craving a taste of Chilean home cooking.

Mariscal

Ingredients:

- 1 lb fresh white fish fillets (such as sea bass or halibut), diced into bite-sized pieces
- 1/2 lb shrimp, peeled and deveined
- 1/2 lb scallops, diced
- 1/2 cup lime juice
- 1/4 cup lemon juice
- 1 red onion, thinly sliced
- 1 red bell pepper, diced
- 1 green bell pepper, diced
- 1-2 jalapeño peppers, seeded and finely chopped
- 1/2 cup chopped fresh cilantro
- 1/4 cup olive oil
- Salt and pepper to taste
- Avocado slices, for garnish
- Plantain chips or crusty bread, for serving

Instructions:

1. Prepare the Seafood:
    - Rinse the fish fillets, shrimp, and scallops under cold water and pat them dry with paper towels. Dice the fish into bite-sized pieces and place all the seafood in a large mixing bowl.
2. Marinate the Seafood:
    - Pour the lime juice and lemon juice over the seafood, making sure it's fully submerged. Cover the bowl with plastic wrap and refrigerate for about 30 minutes to 1 hour, stirring occasionally to ensure all the seafood is evenly marinated. The citrus juices will "cook" the seafood, turning it opaque.
3. Prepare the Vegetables:
    - Meanwhile, thinly slice the red onion, dice the red and green bell peppers, and finely chop the jalapeño peppers. Chop the fresh cilantro.
4. Assemble the Mariscal:
    - Once the seafood is "cooked" in the citrus juices, drain off most of the excess liquid.

- Add the sliced red onion, diced bell peppers, chopped jalapeño peppers, and chopped cilantro to the marinated seafood. Drizzle olive oil over the mixture and gently toss to combine all the ingredients.
- Season with salt and pepper to taste.
5. Chill:
    - Cover the mariscal with plastic wrap and return it to the refrigerator to chill for another 15-30 minutes, allowing the flavors to meld.
6. Serve:
    - To serve, divide the mariscal into individual bowls or glasses. Garnish with slices of avocado.
    - Serve with plantain chips or crusty bread on the side.
7. Enjoy!
Enjoy this delicious and refreshing Mariscal as an appetizer or light meal. The combination of fresh seafood, citrus juices, and aromatic vegetables makes it a delightful dish that's perfect for sharing with family and friends.

Mechada

Ingredients:

- 2 lbs beef chuck roast
- 2 tablespoons vegetable oil
- 1 onion, finely chopped
- 2 carrots, peeled and diced
- 2 stalks celery, diced
- 2 cloves garlic, minced
- 1 cup beef broth
- 1 cup red wine (optional)
- 2 bay leaves
- 1 teaspoon dried oregano
- 1 teaspoon ground cumin
- Salt and pepper to taste

Instructions:

1. Prepare the Beef:
    - Season the beef chuck roast generously with salt and pepper on all sides.
2. Sear the Beef:
    - Heat the vegetable oil in a large Dutch oven or heavy-bottomed pot over medium-high heat. Once hot, add the beef chuck roast and sear on all sides until deeply browned, about 4-5 minutes per side. Remove the beef from the pot and set it aside.
3. Sauté Aromatics:
    - In the same pot, add the chopped onion, diced carrots, diced celery, and minced garlic. Sauté until the vegetables are softened and fragrant, about 5-7 minutes.
4. Deglaze the Pot:
    - Pour in the beef broth and red wine (if using), stirring to scrape up any browned bits from the bottom of the pot.
5. Add Seasonings:
    - Return the seared beef chuck roast to the pot. Add the bay leaves, dried oregano, and ground cumin. Stir to combine.
6. Slow Cook:
    - Cover the pot and reduce the heat to low. Allow the beef to simmer gently for 2-3 hours, or until it is fork-tender and easily shreds apart.

7. Shred the Beef:
   - Once the beef is cooked, remove it from the pot and transfer it to a cutting board. Use two forks to shred the beef into bite-sized pieces.
8. Reduce the Sauce:
   - If desired, return the shredded beef to the pot and simmer uncovered for an additional 10-15 minutes to reduce the sauce and intensify the flavors. Remove and discard the bay leaves.
9. Serve:
   - Serve the mechada hot with rice, mashed potatoes, or as a filling for sandwiches. Garnish with fresh parsley or cilantro if desired.
10. Enjoy!

Mechada is a delicious and comforting dish that's perfect for a hearty meal. Enjoy the tender, flavorful beef and rich sauce with your favorite sides for a satisfying dining experience.

Prietas

Ingredients:

- 1 lb pork blood (fresh or frozen)
- 1/2 lb pork fatback, finely chopped
- 1 cup cooked rice
- 1 onion, finely chopped
- 2 cloves garlic, minced
- 1 tablespoon paprika
- 1 teaspoon ground cumin
- 1 teaspoon dried oregano
- 1/2 teaspoon ground black pepper
- 1/2 teaspoon salt
- 1/4 teaspoon ground cloves
- Casings (natural hog casings or synthetic casings), soaked in water if dried

Instructions:

1. Prepare the Casings:
    - If using dried casings, soak them in warm water for about 30 minutes to soften them. Rinse them thoroughly under cold water to remove any salt or debris. Set aside.
2. Cook the Rice:
    - Cook the rice according to package instructions until tender. Drain any excess water and set the cooked rice aside to cool.
3. Mix the Ingredients:
    - In a large mixing bowl, combine the pork blood, finely chopped pork fatback, cooked rice, chopped onion, minced garlic, paprika, ground cumin, dried oregano, black pepper, salt, and ground cloves. Mix well to combine all the ingredients evenly.
4. Stuff the Casings:
    - Using a sausage stuffer or a funnel, carefully fill the casings with the blood sausage mixture, leaving some space at the ends to tie knots. Avoid overfilling the casings, as they may burst during cooking.
5. Form the Sausages:
    - Once filled, twist the casings at regular intervals to form individual sausages. Use kitchen twine to tie knots at the ends and between each sausage link.

6. Cook the Sausages:
    - There are several methods for cooking prietas:
        - Boiling: Place the sausages in a pot of boiling water and simmer gently for about 20-30 minutes, until cooked through.
        - Grilling: Preheat a grill to medium heat and cook the sausages for 10-15 minutes per side, until browned and cooked through.
        - Pan-Frying: Heat a skillet over medium heat and cook the sausages for 10-15 minutes, turning occasionally, until browned and cooked through.
7. Serve:
    - Once cooked, remove the prietas from the heat and let them rest for a few minutes before serving. Serve hot with bread, chimichurri sauce, or pebre.
8. Enjoy!
   Enjoy your homemade prietas as part of a traditional Chilean barbecue or as a tasty snack or meal. Adjust the seasonings according to your taste preferences, and feel free to experiment with additional spices or ingredients to customize the flavor of your blood sausages.

Mote con Huesillo

Ingredients:

- 1 cup dried peaches (huesillos)
- 1 cup sugar
- 1 cinnamon stick
- 1 cup wheat grains (mote)
- 4 cups water
- Optional: 1/4 teaspoon ground cloves
- Optional: 1/4 teaspoon ground ginger
- Optional: 1/4 teaspoon ground nutmeg

Instructions:

1. Prepare the Dried Peaches (Huesillos):
    - Rinse the dried peaches under cold water to remove any dirt or debris.
    - Place the peaches in a large pot and add enough water to cover them completely.
    - Bring the water to a boil over high heat, then reduce the heat to low and simmer for about 15-20 minutes, or until the peaches are soft and rehydrated.
    - Once soft, remove the peaches from the heat and drain off the water.
2. Make the Syrup:
    - In a separate pot, combine 4 cups of water, sugar, and the cinnamon stick. If using, add the optional ground cloves, ground ginger, and ground nutmeg.
    - Bring the mixture to a boil over medium heat, stirring occasionally to dissolve the sugar.
    - Once the sugar is fully dissolved, reduce the heat to low and simmer the syrup for about 10 minutes to infuse it with the flavors of the spices.
3. Cook the Wheat Grains (Mote):
    - In a separate pot, combine the wheat grains (mote) with enough water to cover them completely.
    - Bring the water to a boil over high heat, then reduce the heat to low and simmer for about 45 minutes to 1 hour, or until the wheat grains are tender.
    - Once tender, drain off any excess water and set the cooked wheat grains aside.

4. Assemble Mote con Huesillo:
   - To assemble the dish, place a few cooked wheat grains (mote) in the bottom of serving glasses or bowls.
   - Add a few rehydrated dried peaches (huesillos) on top of the wheat grains in each glass.
   - Pour the spiced syrup over the wheat grains and peaches until they are fully submerged.
5. Chill and Serve:
   - Refrigerate the assembled mote con huesillo until chilled, about 2-3 hours or overnight.
   - Serve cold, optionally garnished with additional cinnamon sticks or fresh mint leaves.
6. Enjoy!
   Enjoy this refreshing and sweet Chilean treat as a dessert or beverage on a hot summer day. The combination of soft, sweet peaches with tender wheat grains and aromatic spiced syrup is sure to delight your taste buds.

Turrón de Vino

Ingredients:

- 2 cups red wine (such as Cabernet Sauvignon or Merlot)
- 1 cup granulated sugar
- 1/2 cup honey
- 1/2 teaspoon ground cinnamon
- 1/4 teaspoon ground cloves
- 1/4 teaspoon ground nutmeg
- 2 cups mixed nuts (such as almonds, walnuts, and hazelnuts), chopped
- 1 cup raisins
- Vegetable oil, for greasing

Instructions:

1. Prepare the Wine Syrup:
    - In a large saucepan, combine the red wine, granulated sugar, honey, ground cinnamon, ground cloves, and ground nutmeg.
    - Bring the mixture to a boil over medium-high heat, stirring constantly to dissolve the sugar.
    - Once boiling, reduce the heat to low and simmer the syrup for about 15-20 minutes, or until it has thickened slightly and coats the back of a spoon.
2. Toast the Nuts:
    - While the syrup is simmering, spread the chopped nuts on a baking sheet in a single layer.
    - Toast the nuts in a preheated oven at 350°F (175°C) for about 8-10 minutes, or until golden and fragrant. Keep an eye on them to prevent burning.
    - Once toasted, remove the nuts from the oven and set them aside to cool.
3. Combine the Ingredients:
    - Once the wine syrup has thickened, remove it from the heat and let it cool for a few minutes.
    - Stir the toasted nuts and raisins into the warm syrup until evenly coated.
4. Shape the Turrón:
    - Line a baking dish or mold with parchment paper, leaving some overhang for easy removal.
    - Pour the nut and raisin mixture into the prepared dish, pressing it down firmly with a spatula or spoon to compact it.

5. Chill and Set:
    - Place the dish in the refrigerator and chill the turrón for at least 4-6 hours, or until it is firm and set.
6. Slice and Serve:
    - Once chilled and set, use the parchment paper overhang to lift the turrón out of the dish.
    - Place the turrón on a cutting board and slice it into squares or rectangles, depending on your preference.
7. Enjoy!
Enjoy your homemade turrón de vino as a sweet and indulgent treat. Serve it alongside a glass of red wine for an extra special dessert experience. Store any leftovers in an airtight container in the refrigerator for up to a week.

Leche Asada

Ingredients:

- 4 cups whole milk
- 1 cup granulated sugar
- 4 eggs
- 1 teaspoon vanilla extract
- Zest of 1 lemon (optional)
- Ground cinnamon, for garnish (optional)

Instructions:

1. Preheat the Oven:
    - Preheat your oven to 350°F (175°C). Place a large baking dish filled with water on the bottom rack of the oven to create a water bath.
2. Prepare the Custard Mixture:
    - In a saucepan, heat the milk over medium heat until it is hot but not boiling. Remove from heat and let it cool slightly.
    - In a separate bowl, beat the eggs and sugar together until well combined.
    - Gradually add the warm milk to the egg mixture, whisking continuously to prevent the eggs from scrambling.
    - Stir in the vanilla extract and lemon zest, if using. Mix until smooth.
3. Strain the Mixture:
    - Strain the custard mixture through a fine-mesh sieve to remove any lumps or air bubbles.
4. Bake the Leche Asada:
    - Pour the strained custard mixture into a greased baking dish or individual ramekins.
    - Place the baking dish or ramekins in the preheated oven, making sure they are sitting in the water bath.
    - Bake for about 45-50 minutes, or until the custard is set and the top is lightly golden brown.
5. Chill and Serve:
    - Remove the leche asada from the oven and let it cool to room temperature.
    - Once cooled, cover the dish or ramekins with plastic wrap and refrigerate for at least 2 hours, or until thoroughly chilled and set.
6. Garnish and Serve:

- To serve, sprinkle the top of the leche asada with ground cinnamon, if desired.
- Cut into squares if baked in a large dish, or serve individually if baked in ramekins.

7. Enjoy!
Enjoy this creamy and delicious leche asada as a delightful dessert after a meal or as a sweet treat any time of day. Its rich flavor and smooth texture are sure to be a hit with family and friends.

Crudos

Ingredients:

- 1/2 lb beef tenderloin or sirloin, very finely chopped or minced
- 1 small onion, finely chopped
- 1 tablespoon fresh lemon juice
- 1 tablespoon olive oil
- 1 teaspoon Worcestershire sauce
- Salt and pepper, to taste
- Optional garnishes: chopped parsley, diced tomatoes, capers, sliced radishes, sliced onions, sliced jalapeños

Instructions:

1. Prepare the Beef:
    - Start by ensuring that your beef is very fresh and of high quality. It's essential to use beef that is suitable for raw consumption, such as tenderloin or sirloin.
    - Trim any excess fat from the beef and finely chop or mince it with a sharp knife. You can also use a meat grinder if you prefer a smoother texture.
2. Season the Beef:
    - In a mixing bowl, combine the finely chopped beef with the chopped onion, fresh lemon juice, olive oil, and Worcestershire sauce.
    - Season the mixture with salt and pepper to taste. Be sure to taste and adjust the seasoning as needed.
3. Mix Well:
    - Use a spoon or your hands to mix the ingredients together thoroughly, ensuring that the seasonings are evenly distributed throughout the beef mixture.
4. Chill:
    - Once mixed, cover the bowl with plastic wrap and refrigerate the crudos for at least 30 minutes to allow the flavors to meld together and for the beef to chill slightly.
5. Serve:
    - To serve, divide the chilled crudos into individual portions and arrange them on serving plates.

    - Optionally, garnish the crudos with chopped parsley, diced tomatoes, capers, sliced radishes, sliced onions, or sliced jalapeños for added flavor and presentation.
6. Enjoy!
Enjoy your homemade crudos as a delicious appetizer or snack. Serve them with crusty bread, crackers, or toasted baguette slices for spreading. Be sure to enjoy them promptly after preparation for the best flavor and texture.

Cola de Mono

Ingredients:

- 2 cups milk
- 1 cup water
- 1 cup sugar
- 1 cinnamon stick
- 4 cloves
- 1 tablespoon instant coffee granules
- 1 teaspoon vanilla extract
- 1/2 cup rum (optional)
- Ground cinnamon, for garnish (optional)

Instructions:

1. Prepare the Spiced Syrup:
    - In a saucepan, combine the milk, water, sugar, cinnamon stick, and cloves.
    - Heat the mixture over medium heat, stirring occasionally, until the sugar is dissolved and the mixture is hot but not boiling.
2. Infuse the Flavors:
    - Once the mixture is hot, add the instant coffee granules and vanilla extract.
    - Continue to heat the mixture for another 5 minutes, allowing the flavors to infuse. Stir occasionally.
3. Strain and Cool:
    - Remove the saucepan from the heat and strain the mixture through a fine-mesh sieve to remove the spices.
    - Let the spiced syrup cool to room temperature. You can transfer it to a pitcher or container for easier serving.
4. Add Rum (Optional):
    - If using rum, stir it into the cooled spiced syrup. Adjust the amount of rum according to your preference for alcohol content.
5. Chill:
    - Once the rum is added (if using), refrigerate the Cola de Mono until thoroughly chilled, about 1-2 hours.
6. Serve:
    - To serve, pour the chilled Cola de Mono into glasses over ice.
    - Optionally, sprinkle ground cinnamon on top of each glass for garnish.

- Transfer the crab mixture to the greased baking dish, spreading it out evenly.
6. **Bake:**
    - Place the baking dish in the preheated oven and bake for 30-35 minutes, or until the top is golden brown and the mixture is heated through.
7. **Serve:**
    - Once baked, remove the pastel de jaiba from the oven and let it cool for a few minutes before slicing.
    - Serve warm as a main dish or appetizer, garnished with additional chopped cilantro if desired.
8. **Enjoy!**
   Enjoy the delicious flavors of this traditional Chilean dish. Pastel de Jaiba is perfect for a family dinner or special occasion, and it pairs well with a fresh salad or crusty bread.

Pollo al Cognac

Ingredients:

- 4 boneless, skinless chicken breasts
- Salt and pepper to taste
- 2 tablespoons olive oil
- 2 tablespoons butter
- 1 onion, finely chopped
- 2 cloves garlic, minced
- 8 oz (225g) mushrooms, sliced
- 1/4 cup Cognac or brandy
- 1 cup chicken broth
- 1/2 cup heavy cream
- 1 tablespoon Dijon mustard
- 1 tablespoon fresh thyme leaves
- Chopped fresh parsley, for garnish

Instructions:

1. Prepare the Chicken:
   - Season the chicken breasts with salt and pepper on both sides.
2. Sear the Chicken:
   - In a large skillet, heat the olive oil and butter over medium-high heat. Add the chicken breasts and cook for 4-5 minutes on each side, or until golden brown and cooked through. Remove the chicken from the skillet and set aside.
3. Cook the Aromatics:
   - In the same skillet, add the chopped onion and cook for 2-3 minutes until softened. Add the minced garlic and cook for another minute until fragrant.
4. Add Mushrooms and Deglaze:
   - Add the sliced mushrooms to the skillet and cook for 5-6 minutes, or until they are golden brown and tender. Pour in the Cognac or brandy and let it cook for 1-2 minutes to deglaze the skillet, scraping up any browned bits from the bottom.
5. Simmer with Broth and Cream:

- Pour in the chicken broth and bring the mixture to a simmer. Let it cook for 2-3 minutes to reduce slightly. Stir in the heavy cream and Dijon mustard, and simmer for another 2-3 minutes until the sauce thickens slightly.

6. Return Chicken to Skillet:
    - Return the chicken breasts to the skillet and spoon some of the sauce over the top. Cook for another 2-3 minutes, allowing the chicken to heat through and absorb the flavors of the sauce.
7. Finish and Garnish:
    - Sprinkle fresh thyme leaves over the chicken and sauce. Garnish with chopped fresh parsley before serving.
8. Serve:
    - Serve the Pollo al Cognac hot, accompanied by your favorite side dishes such as mashed potatoes, rice, or steamed vegetables.
9. Enjoy!
   Enjoy this delicious and elegant chicken dish with the rich and creamy cognac sauce. It's perfect for a special dinner or entertaining guests.

Chapalele

Ingredients:

- 2 cups mashed potatoes (about 3-4 medium potatoes, boiled and mashed)
- 1 cup flour
- 1 teaspoon salt
- Water (as needed)

Instructions:

1. Prepare the Potatoes:
    - Peel the potatoes and cut them into small chunks.
    - Boil the potatoes in salted water until they are soft.
    - Drain the potatoes and mash them thoroughly. Let them cool slightly.
2. Make the Dough:
    - In a large mixing bowl, combine the mashed potatoes, flour, and salt.
    - Mix well until a dough forms. If the dough is too sticky, gradually add more flour until it becomes manageable.
3. Form the Chapalele:
    - Dust a clean surface with flour.
    - Take a portion of the dough and roll it into a rope about 1 inch thick.
    - Cut the rope into small pieces, about 1 to 1.5 inches in length.
    - Optionally, you can shape the pieces by rolling them gently between your palms or pressing them lightly with a fork to create ridges.
4. Cook the Chapalele:
    - Bring a large pot of salted water to a boil.
    - Carefully drop the chapalele into the boiling water, a few at a time, making sure not to overcrowd the pot.
    - Cook the chapalele for about 5-7 minutes, or until they float to the surface.
    - Remove the cooked chapalele with a slotted spoon and transfer them to a plate.
5. Serve:
    - Chapalele can be served with a variety of toppings or sauces. Traditionally, they are served with a simple tomato sauce, or with grated cheese and butter.
    - Enjoy your homemade chapalele!

Feel free to adjust the seasoning or add your own twist to this recipe to suit your taste preferences!

Pastel de Papas

Ingredients:

- 2 lbs (about 1 kg) potatoes, peeled and thinly sliced
- 1 lb (about 500 g) ground beef
- 1 large onion, finely chopped
- 2 cloves garlic, minced
- 1 teaspoon paprika
- Salt and pepper to taste
- 2 tablespoons vegetable oil
- 1 cup beef or vegetable broth
- 2 boiled eggs, sliced (optional)
- 1 cup shredded cheese (cheddar, mozzarella, or any melting cheese)
- Butter for greasing the baking dish

Instructions:

1. Preheat the Oven:
    - Preheat your oven to 375°F (190°C).
2. Prepare the Potatoes:
    - Peel the potatoes and thinly slice them. You can use a mandoline slicer for uniform slices, if available.
    - Place the sliced potatoes in a bowl of cold water to prevent them from browning.
3. Cook the Ground Beef:
    - Heat the vegetable oil in a large skillet over medium heat.
    - Add the chopped onions and garlic, and sauté until softened and translucent.
    - Add the ground beef to the skillet, breaking it apart with a spoon, and cook until browned.
    - Season the beef with paprika, salt, and pepper to taste.
    - Pour in the beef or vegetable broth and simmer for a few minutes until the liquid reduces slightly. Remove from heat and set aside.
4. Assemble the Pastel de Papas:
    - Grease a baking dish with butter.
    - Drain the sliced potatoes and pat them dry with paper towels.
    - Arrange a layer of sliced potatoes on the bottom of the baking dish, slightly overlapping them.

- Spread half of the cooked ground beef mixture evenly over the potato layer.
- If using, arrange the sliced boiled eggs on top of the beef layer.
- Sprinkle half of the shredded cheese over the beef and egg layer.
- Repeat the layers: sliced potatoes, remaining beef mixture, and remaining cheese.

5. Bake the Pastel de Papas:
   - Cover the baking dish with aluminum foil and bake in the preheated oven for 45 minutes.
   - Remove the foil and bake for an additional 15-20 minutes, or until the top is golden brown and the potatoes are tender when pierced with a fork.
6. Serve:
   - Allow the pastel de papas to cool for a few minutes before slicing and serving.
   - Enjoy this comforting and flavorful dish with a side salad or on its own!

Feel free to adjust the seasonings and ingredients according to your taste preferences. Pastel de papas is a versatile dish, and you can customize it with additional vegetables or spices to suit your liking.

Berlín

Ingredients:

- 2 1/4 teaspoons (1 packet) active dry yeast
- 1/4 cup warm water
- 3/4 cup warm milk
- 1/4 cup granulated sugar
- 1 teaspoon salt
- 1/4 cup unsalted butter, melted
- 2 large eggs
- 4 cups all-purpose flour (approximately)
- Oil for frying
- Jam, dulce de leche, or custard for filling
- Powdered sugar for dusting

Instructions:

1. Activate the Yeast:
   - In a small bowl, dissolve the yeast in warm water. Let it sit for about 5-10 minutes until it becomes frothy.
2. Prepare the Dough:
   - In a large mixing bowl, combine the warm milk, sugar, salt, melted butter, and eggs. Mix well.
   - Add the activated yeast mixture to the bowl and stir to combine.
   - Gradually add the flour, mixing until a soft dough forms. You may not need to use all the flour.
   - Knead the dough on a lightly floured surface for about 5-7 minutes until it's smooth and elastic.
3. First Rise:
   - Place the dough in a greased bowl, cover it with a clean kitchen towel or plastic wrap, and let it rise in a warm place for about 1-2 hours, or until it doubles in size.
4. Shape and Fill the Berlínes:
   - Punch down the risen dough and divide it into equal-sized portions.
   - Flatten each portion into a circle and place a spoonful of jam, dulce de leche, or custard in the center.
   - Fold the dough over the filling and pinch the edges to seal, forming a ball.
5. Second Rise:

- Place the filled berlínes on a baking sheet lined with parchment paper, leaving some space between them.
- Cover the berlínes with a clean kitchen towel or plastic wrap and let them rise again for about 30-45 minutes.

6. Fry the Berlínes:
    - Heat oil in a deep fryer or heavy-bottomed pot to 350°F (175°C).
    - Carefully place the risen berlínes into the hot oil, a few at a time, and fry until golden brown on both sides, turning them halfway through. It should take about 3-4 minutes per side.
    - Remove the fried berlínes from the oil and drain them on paper towels to remove excess oil.
7. Finish and Serve:
    - Dust the warm berlínes with powdered sugar.
    - Serve them fresh and enjoy the delightful combination of crispy exterior and sweet, gooey filling.

Berlínes are best enjoyed fresh on the day they're made, but they can also be stored in an airtight container at room temperature for up to 2 days.

Torta de Mil Hojas

Ingredients:

For the Puff Pastry:

- 2 sheets of puff pastry (store-bought or homemade)

For the Pastry Cream:

- 2 cups whole milk
- 4 egg yolks
- 1/2 cup granulated sugar
- 1/4 cup cornstarch
- 1 teaspoon vanilla extract

For Assembly:

- Powdered sugar, for dusting (optional)
- Chocolate glaze (optional)

Instructions:

1. Prepare the Puff Pastry:

- If using store-bought puff pastry, follow the package instructions for thawing.
- If making homemade puff pastry, roll out the pastry sheets on a lightly floured surface to about 1/8-inch thickness. Prick the pastry with a fork to prevent it from puffing up too much during baking.
- Cut the pastry into rectangles of equal size (usually about 3x3 inches). Place the rectangles on a baking sheet lined with parchment paper.
- Bake the pastry according to the package instructions or until golden brown and puffed. Let them cool completely.

2. Make the Pastry Cream:

- In a saucepan, heat the milk over medium heat until it just begins to simmer. Remove from heat.
- In a separate bowl, whisk together the egg yolks, sugar, and cornstarch until smooth and pale yellow.
- Slowly pour the hot milk into the egg mixture, whisking constantly to prevent the eggs from curdling.

- Return the mixture to the saucepan and cook over medium heat, stirring constantly, until it thickens and comes to a gentle boil. This should take about 2-3 minutes.
- Remove the pastry cream from the heat and stir in the vanilla extract.
- Transfer the pastry cream to a bowl and cover it with plastic wrap, pressing the wrap directly onto the surface of the cream to prevent a skin from forming. Refrigerate until completely chilled.

3. Assemble the Torta de Mil Hojas:

- Place one layer of puff pastry on a serving plate or cake stand.
- Spread a generous layer of pastry cream over the pastry.
- Top with another layer of puff pastry and repeat the process until you've used all the pastry and cream, ending with a layer of pastry on top.
- If desired, spread a thin layer of pastry cream over the top layer of pastry for a smoother finish.
- Optional: Prepare a chocolate glaze by melting chocolate with a bit of butter or cream, and pour it over the top layer of pastry.
- Refrigerate the torta for at least 1-2 hours before serving to allow the flavors to meld and the pastry cream to set.
- Before serving, dust the top of the torta with powdered sugar, if desired.
- Slice and serve the Torta de Mil Hojas, enjoying the delicate layers of pastry and creamy filling.

This dessert is best enjoyed chilled and can be stored in the refrigerator for up to 2-3 days.

Sopa de Cola de Mono

Ingredients:

- 2 lbs (about 1 kg) beef tail, cut into pieces
- 1 onion, chopped
- 2 carrots, diced
- 2 celery stalks, diced
- 2 cloves garlic, minced
- 1 leek, chopped
- 2 bay leaves
- 1 teaspoon dried thyme
- 1 teaspoon dried oregano
- Salt and pepper to taste
- 8 cups beef broth or water
- 2 tablespoons vegetable oil
- Chopped fresh parsley for garnish (optional)

Instructions:

1. Prepare the Beef Tail:
    - Rinse the beef tail pieces under cold water and pat them dry with paper towels.
    - Season the beef tail with salt and pepper.
2. Sear the Beef Tail:
    - Heat the vegetable oil in a large pot or Dutch oven over medium-high heat.
    - Add the beef tail pieces to the pot and sear them on all sides until browned. This will help develop flavor in the soup.
    - Remove the beef tail from the pot and set it aside.
3. Saute the Vegetables:
    - In the same pot, add the chopped onion, carrots, celery, garlic, and leek.
    - Saute the vegetables for 5-7 minutes, or until they begin to soften.
4. Simmer the Soup:
    - Return the seared beef tail pieces to the pot.
    - Add the bay leaves, dried thyme, dried oregano, and beef broth or water.
    - Bring the soup to a boil, then reduce the heat to low and let it simmer, covered, for 2-3 hours, or until the beef tail is tender and falling off the bone.

- Skim off any foam or impurities that rise to the surface of the soup during cooking.
5. Serve:
    - Once the beef tail is tender, remove it from the pot and shred the meat using a fork. Discard any bones and excess fat.
    - Return the shredded beef tail meat to the pot.
    - Taste the soup and adjust the seasoning with salt and pepper, if needed.
    - Ladle the Sopa de Cola de Mono into bowls and garnish with chopped fresh parsley, if desired.
    - Serve hot and enjoy this comforting and flavorful Chilean soup!

Feel free to customize this recipe by adding other vegetables or herbs according to your taste preferences. Sopa de Cola de Mono pairs well with crusty bread or rice for a complete meal.

Ensalada a la Chilena

Ingredients:

- 3 large tomatoes, sliced
- 1 large onion, thinly sliced
- 1 tablespoon fresh cilantro, chopped (optional)
- 1 tablespoon olive oil
- 1 tablespoon red wine vinegar
- Salt and pepper to taste

Instructions:

1. Prepare the Vegetables:
    - Wash the tomatoes and slice them into rounds.
    - Peel and thinly slice the onion.
2. Assemble the Salad:
    - Arrange the tomato slices on a serving platter.
    - Scatter the sliced onions over the tomatoes.
    - Sprinkle the chopped cilantro (if using) over the salad.
3. Season the Salad:
    - Drizzle the olive oil and red wine vinegar over the salad.
    - Season with salt and pepper to taste.
4. Serve:
    - Serve the Ensalada a la Chilena immediately as a side dish alongside your main course.
    - Enjoy the fresh and vibrant flavors of this traditional Chilean salad!

This salad is versatile and can be customized to your taste preferences. You can add other ingredients such as sliced bell peppers, avocado, or olives if you like. Additionally, some variations of Ensalada a la Chilena include adding a sprinkle of oregano or a squeeze of lemon juice for extra flavor.

Milcaos

Ingredients:

- 4 large potatoes (preferably a starchy variety like Russet), peeled and grated
- 2 large potatoes, boiled and mashed
- 2 tablespoons wheat flour (optional, for binding)
- Salt to taste
- 2 tablespoons lard or vegetable oil (for frying)
- Water (as needed)
- Optional: pork cracklings (chicharrones) for added flavor and texture

Instructions:

1. Prepare the Potatoes:
    - Peel the potatoes and grate them using a box grater or food processor.
    - Place the grated potatoes in a clean kitchen towel or cheesecloth and squeeze out any excess moisture.
2. Make the Milcao Batter:
    - In a mixing bowl, combine the grated potatoes, mashed potatoes, and wheat flour (if using).
    - Season the mixture with salt to taste and mix well. If the mixture seems too dry, you can add a little water to moisten it.
3. Form the Milcaos:
    - Take a portion of the potato mixture and shape it into a flat pancake, about 1/2 to 3/4 inch thick.
    - Optionally, you can press pork cracklings into the surface of the milcao for added flavor and texture.
4. Cook the Milcaos:
    - Heat the lard or vegetable oil in a large skillet or frying pan over medium heat.
    - Carefully place the milcaos in the hot oil and cook them for about 5-7 minutes on each side, or until they are golden brown and crispy.
    - You may need to cook the milcaos in batches, depending on the size of your skillet.
5. Serve:
    - Once cooked, transfer the milcaos to a plate lined with paper towels to drain any excess oil.
    - Serve the milcaos hot as a side dish or as part of a main meal.

- Enjoy the deliciously crispy and flavorful potato pancakes!

Milcaos can be enjoyed on their own or served with toppings such as sour cream, salsa, or ají (Chilean hot sauce) for extra flavor. They are best served fresh and hot, but any leftovers can be stored in an airtight container in the refrigerator and reheated in a skillet or oven before serving.

Caldillo de Congrio a la Chilena

Ingredients:

- 1 1/2 lbs (about 700g) congrio fillets, cut into large chunks
- 1 onion, chopped
- 2 carrots, diced
- 2 potatoes, peeled and diced
- 1 bell pepper, diced
- 2 tomatoes, diced
- 2 cloves garlic, minced
- 1/4 cup chopped fresh cilantro
- 1 teaspoon paprika
- 1/2 teaspoon ground cumin
- 1/2 teaspoon dried oregano
- 6 cups fish or vegetable broth
- 1/4 cup white wine (optional)
- Salt and pepper to taste
- Olive oil for cooking
- Lemon wedges for serving

Instructions:

1. Prepare the Congrio:
    - Rinse the congrio fillets under cold water and pat them dry with paper towels. Cut the fillets into large chunks and set them aside.
2. Saute the Vegetables:
    - Heat a drizzle of olive oil in a large pot over medium heat.
    - Add the chopped onion, carrots, potatoes, bell pepper, and garlic to the pot.
    - Saute the vegetables for 5-7 minutes, or until they begin to soften.
3. Add the Seasonings:
    - Stir in the paprika, ground cumin, and dried oregano, and cook for another minute to toast the spices and release their flavors.
4. Simmer the Soup:
    - Pour the fish or vegetable broth into the pot and bring the mixture to a simmer.
    - Add the diced tomatoes and chopped cilantro to the pot.
    - If using, pour in the white wine.

- Season the soup with salt and pepper to taste.
- Let the soup simmer gently for about 15-20 minutes, or until the vegetables are tender and the flavors have melded together.

5. Add the Congrio:
    - Carefully add the chunks of congrio fillets to the pot.
    - Let the soup simmer for an additional 5-7 minutes, or until the fish is cooked through and flakes easily with a fork.
6. Serve:
    - Ladle the Caldillo de Congrio into bowls.
    - Serve hot, garnished with additional chopped cilantro and accompanied by lemon wedges for squeezing over the soup.
    - Enjoy this delicious and comforting Chilean fish soup with crusty bread or rice on the side!

Caldillo de Congrio is a versatile dish, and you can customize it by adding other vegetables or seasonings according to your taste preferences. It's best enjoyed fresh and hot, but any leftovers can be stored in an airtight container in the refrigerator for up to 2-3 days.

Leche Nevada

Ingredients:

For the Custard:

- 4 cups whole milk
- 1/2 cup granulated sugar
- 4 egg yolks
- 1 teaspoon vanilla extract
- Zest of 1 lemon (optional)

For the Meringue:

- 4 egg whites
- 1/2 cup granulated sugar
- Pinch of cream of tartar (optional)

For Garnish:

- Ground cinnamon or nutmeg (optional)

Instructions:

1. Prepare the Custard:

   1. In a saucepan, heat the milk over medium heat until it just begins to simmer. Do not boil.
   2. In a separate bowl, whisk together the egg yolks and sugar until well combined.
   3. Gradually pour the hot milk into the egg yolk mixture, whisking constantly to prevent the eggs from curdling.
   4. Return the mixture to the saucepan and cook over medium-low heat, stirring constantly, until it thickens and coats the back of a spoon. This should take about 8-10 minutes.
   5. Remove the custard from the heat and stir in the vanilla extract and lemon zest, if using. Let it cool slightly.

2. Make the Meringue:

   1. In a clean, dry mixing bowl, beat the egg whites with an electric mixer on medium speed until foamy.
   2. Add a pinch of cream of tartar (if using) to stabilize the meringue.

3. Gradually add the granulated sugar, a spoonful at a time, while continuing to beat the egg whites. Beat until stiff peaks form and the meringue is glossy.

3. Assemble the Leche Nevada:

   1. Pour the slightly cooled custard into a serving dish or individual dessert cups.
   2. Using a spoon or spatula, gently dollop the meringue on top of the custard, creating small mounds or "islands."
   3. Optionally, you can use a kitchen torch to lightly toast the meringue for added flavor and color.
   4. Sprinkle ground cinnamon or nutmeg over the top for garnish, if desired.
   5. Chill the Leche Nevada in the refrigerator for at least 1-2 hours before serving to allow the flavors to meld and the meringue to set.

4. Serve:

   1. Serve the Leche Nevada cold as a refreshing and delightful dessert.
   2. Enjoy the creamy custard topped with light and airy meringue clouds!

Leche Nevada is a beautiful and elegant dessert that is sure to impress your guests. Feel free to customize it by adding other flavorings such as orange zest, almond extract, or a splash of rum to the custard.

Pastel de Choclo a la Chilena

Ingredients:

For the Filling:

- 1 lb (450g) ground beef
- 1 onion, chopped
- 2 cloves garlic, minced
- 1 tablespoon vegetable oil
- 1 teaspoon ground cumin
- 1 teaspoon paprika
- Salt and pepper to taste
- 1 cup cooked chicken, shredded (optional)
- 1/2 cup pitted black olives, sliced
- 2 hard-boiled eggs, sliced
- 1/4 cup raisins (optional)
- 1/4 cup chopped fresh parsley

For the Corn Topping:

- 6 cups fresh or canned corn kernels
- 1 cup milk
- 2 tablespoons butter
- 1 tablespoon granulated sugar
- Salt to taste

Instructions:

1. Prepare the Filling:

   1. Heat the vegetable oil in a large skillet over medium heat. Add the chopped onion and garlic, and cook until softened.
   2. Add the ground beef to the skillet and cook until browned, breaking it apart with a spoon as it cooks.
   3. Stir in the ground cumin, paprika, salt, and pepper. Cook for another minute to toast the spices.
   4. If using, add the cooked shredded chicken to the skillet, along with the sliced olives, raisins, and chopped parsley. Mix well to combine. Remove from heat and set aside.

2. Prepare the Corn Topping:

    1. If using fresh corn, remove the kernels from the cobs. If using canned corn, drain the corn kernels.
    2. In a blender or food processor, blend half of the corn kernels with the milk until smooth.
    3. In a large saucepan, melt the butter over medium heat. Add the blended corn mixture, remaining corn kernels, granulated sugar, and salt. Cook, stirring occasionally, until the mixture thickens, about 10-15 minutes. Remove from heat and let it cool slightly.

3. Assemble and Bake the Pastel de Choclo:

    1. Preheat your oven to 375°F (190°C). Grease a baking dish with butter or oil.
    2. Spread half of the corn mixture evenly on the bottom of the prepared baking dish.
    3. Arrange the cooked beef and chicken mixture over the corn layer.
    4. Top the filling with the sliced hard-boiled eggs.
    5. Cover the filling with the remaining corn mixture, spreading it out evenly.
    6. Bake the Pastel de Choclo in the preheated oven for 40-45 minutes, or until the corn topping is golden brown and crispy.
    7. Remove from the oven and let it cool for a few minutes before serving.

4. Serve:

    1. Serve the Pastel de Choclo hot, either as a main dish or as part of a larger meal.
    2. Enjoy the delicious flavors of this classic Chilean dish!

Feel free to customize the filling with other ingredients such as diced bell peppers, peas, or carrots, according to your taste preferences. Pastel de Choclo is a versatile dish that can be adapted to suit your liking.

Sopaipillas Pasadas

Ingredients:

For the Sopaipillas:

- 2 cups pumpkin or squash puree
- 3 cups all-purpose flour
- 1 teaspoon baking powder
- 1/2 teaspoon salt
- Vegetable oil for frying

For the Syrup:

- 2 cups water
- 1 1/2 cups brown sugar or piloncillo (unrefined cane sugar)
- 1 cinnamon stick
- 1 orange peel (optional)
- 1 teaspoon ground cinnamon (optional)
- 1/2 teaspoon ground cloves (optional)

Instructions:

1. Prepare the Sopaipillas:

    1. In a large mixing bowl, combine the pumpkin or squash puree with the flour, baking powder, and salt. Mix well to form a smooth dough. If the dough is too sticky, you can add a little more flour.
    2. On a floured surface, roll out the dough to about 1/4 inch thickness.
    3. Use a knife or pastry cutter to cut the dough into rounds or squares, about 3-4 inches in diameter.
    4. Heat vegetable oil in a deep fryer or large skillet to 350°F (175°C).
    5. Carefully add the sopaipillas to the hot oil, a few at a time, and fry until golden brown on both sides, about 2-3 minutes per side.
    6. Remove the sopaipillas from the oil and drain them on paper towels to remove excess oil.

2. Prepare the Syrup:

    1. In a saucepan, combine the water, brown sugar or piloncillo, cinnamon stick, and orange peel (if using).

2. Bring the mixture to a boil over medium heat, stirring occasionally to dissolve the sugar.
3. Reduce the heat to low and let the syrup simmer for about 15-20 minutes, or until it thickens slightly.
4. If desired, stir in ground cinnamon and ground cloves for additional flavor.

3. Serve the Sopaipillas Pasadas:

1. Place the fried sopaipillas in a serving dish.
2. Pour the warm syrup over the sopaipillas, allowing them to soak up the syrup.
3. Let the sopaipillas pasadas sit for a few minutes to absorb the syrup before serving.
4. Optionally, sprinkle ground cinnamon over the top for garnish.
5. Serve the sopaipillas pasadas warm and enjoy this delicious Chilean dessert!

Sopaipillas Pasadas are best enjoyed fresh, but any leftovers can be stored in an airtight container in the refrigerator. Reheat them gently in the microwave or oven before serving.

Sopa de Cazuela

Ingredients:

For the Broth:

- 8 cups beef or chicken broth (homemade or store-bought)
- 1 onion, peeled and halved
- 2 carrots, peeled and chopped
- 2 celery stalks, chopped
- 2 cloves garlic, peeled and smashed
- 2 bay leaves
- Salt and pepper to taste

For the Stew:

- 1 lb (about 450g) beef stew meat, cut into bite-sized pieces
- 1 lb (about 450g) bone-in chicken pieces (such as thighs or drumsticks)
- 1 cup diced pumpkin or squash
- 1 cup diced potatoes
- 1 cup diced carrots
- 1 cup diced zucchini
- 1 cup diced green beans
- 1/2 cup rice or pearl barley (optional)
- 1/2 cup frozen peas (optional)
- Chopped fresh cilantro or parsley for garnish (optional)

Instructions:

1. Prepare the Broth:

    1. In a large soup pot or Dutch oven, combine the beef or chicken broth with the halved onion, chopped carrots, celery, smashed garlic cloves, and bay leaves.
    2. Season with salt and pepper to taste.
    3. Bring the broth to a boil over medium-high heat, then reduce the heat to low and let it simmer gently for about 30 minutes to allow the flavors to develop.

2. Brown the Meats (Optional):

1. If desired, you can brown the beef stew meat and chicken pieces before adding them to the broth. Heat a drizzle of oil in a separate skillet over medium-high heat and brown the meat on all sides. This step adds extra flavor to the soup.

3. Add the Meat and Vegetables:

    1. Once the broth has simmered for about 30 minutes, add the browned meat (if using) to the pot.
    2. Add the diced pumpkin or squash, potatoes, carrots, zucchini, and green beans to the pot.
    3. If using rice or pearl barley, add it to the pot at this time.
    4. Bring the soup back to a simmer and let it cook, uncovered, for about 30-40 minutes, or until the meat is tender and the vegetables are cooked through.

4. Finish and Serve:

    1. If using frozen peas, add them to the pot during the last 5 minutes of cooking.
    2. Taste the soup and adjust the seasoning with salt and pepper, if needed.
    3. Ladle the Sopa de Cazuela into bowls and garnish with chopped fresh cilantro or parsley, if desired.
    4. Serve hot and enjoy this delicious and comforting Chilean stew!

Sopa de Cazuela is a versatile dish, and you can customize it by adding other vegetables or herbs according to your taste preferences. It's best enjoyed fresh and hot, and any leftovers can be stored in an airtight container in the refrigerator for up to 3-4 days. Reheat gently on the stovetop or in the microwave before serving.

Piure

Ingredients:

- Fresh piure (sea squirt or sea pineapple)
- Lemon wedges (optional)
- Salt (optional)

Instructions:

1. Cleaning the Piure (if necessary):
    - Rinse the piure under cold water to remove any sand or debris that may be attached to its surface.
2. Serving Fresh:
    - Piure can be enjoyed fresh as a standalone dish. Simply place the cleaned piure on a plate and serve it as is.
    - Optionally, squeeze some fresh lemon juice over the piure for added flavor.
3. Enhancing Flavor (optional):
    - If desired, you can sprinkle a small amount of salt over the piure to enhance its natural flavor. However, be cautious with the amount of salt since piure already has a naturally salty taste.
4. Enjoying Piure:
    - Piure can be eaten raw or lightly cooked, depending on your preference. Some people enjoy its unique texture and flavor without any additional cooking.
5. Incorporating into Recipes (optional):
    - If you prefer to incorporate piure into recipes, you can add it to seafood salads, ceviche, or seafood pasta dishes.
    - Piure can also be used as a garnish or topping for seafood appetizers or sushi rolls.
6. Serving Suggestions:
    - Serve the prepared piure as part of a seafood platter or appetizer spread, accompanied by other fresh seafood and dipping sauces.
    - Enjoy piure with crusty bread or crackers to complement its flavor and texture.
7. Note:
    - Since piure is primarily harvested from the ocean, it's essential to ensure that it comes from clean and unpolluted waters to avoid contamination and foodborne illnesses.

Additional Tips:

- If you're unable to find fresh piure, you may be able to find frozen or preserved sea squirt or sea pineapple at specialty seafood markets or online.
- When purchasing piure or its equivalent, ensure that it's sourced from reputable suppliers and properly stored to maintain freshness and quality.

Enjoy experimenting with piure and incorporating it into your culinary creations to experience its unique taste and texture!

Machas a la Parmesana

Ingredients:

- 1 lb (about 450g) fresh machas (razor clams), cleaned and shelled
- 2 tablespoons butter
- 2 cloves garlic, minced
- 1/4 cup white wine
- 1/2 cup heavy cream
- 1/2 cup grated Parmesan cheese
- Salt and pepper to taste
- Fresh parsley, chopped, for garnish
- Lemon wedges, for serving
- Bread or crackers, for serving (optional)

Instructions:

1. Preheat the Oven:
    - Preheat your oven to 400°F (200°C).
2. Prepare the Machas:
    - Clean the machas by rinsing them under cold water and removing any grit or sand.
    - If the machas are still in their shells, shuck them carefully and discard the shells. Alternatively, you can purchase shelled machas from the seafood market.
3. Prepare the Sauce:
    - In a skillet or frying pan, melt the butter over medium heat.
    - Add the minced garlic to the pan and sauté for 1-2 minutes, or until fragrant.
    - Pour in the white wine and simmer for another 1-2 minutes to cook off the alcohol.
    - Stir in the heavy cream and grated Parmesan cheese, and cook until the sauce thickens slightly, about 2-3 minutes.
    - Season the sauce with salt and pepper to taste.
4. Cook the Machas:
    - Add the cleaned machas to the skillet with the sauce, tossing gently to coat them in the sauce.
    - Cook the machas in the sauce for 2-3 minutes, or until they are heated through.

5. Assemble and Bake:
    - Transfer the machas and sauce to an oven-safe baking dish or individual ramekins.
    - Sprinkle additional Parmesan cheese on top, if desired.
    - Place the baking dish or ramekins in the preheated oven and bake for 5-7 minutes, or until the cheese is melted and bubbly.
6. Garnish and Serve:
    - Remove the machas a la Parmesana from the oven and garnish with chopped fresh parsley.
    - Serve hot, accompanied by lemon wedges for squeezing over the machas.
    - Optionally, serve with bread or crackers on the side for dipping into the creamy sauce.
7. Enjoy!
    - Enjoy the delicious flavors of Machas a la Parmesana as a flavorful appetizer or main course.

This dish is best enjoyed immediately while the cheese is still warm and gooey. It pairs well with a crisp white wine or a light salad for a complete meal.

Pantrucas

Ingredients:

For the Pantrucas:

- 2 cups all-purpose flour
- 1/2 teaspoon salt
- 1/2 cup water (or more as needed)
- 1 egg (optional)
- 1 tablespoon vegetable oil

For the Soup:

- 6 cups chicken or beef broth (homemade or store-bought)
- 1 onion, chopped
- 2 carrots, diced
- 2 celery stalks, diced
- 2 cloves garlic, minced
- 1 teaspoon dried oregano
- 1 teaspoon dried thyme
- Salt and pepper to taste
- Chopped fresh parsley for garnish (optional)

Instructions:

1. Prepare the Pantrucas Dough:

    1. In a mixing bowl, combine the all-purpose flour and salt.
    2. If using, add the egg to the bowl and mix until well combined.
    3. Gradually add the water to the flour mixture, stirring continuously, until a smooth dough forms. You may need to adjust the amount of water to achieve the right consistency.
    4. Knead the dough on a floured surface for a few minutes until it becomes elastic and smooth.
    5. Divide the dough into small portions and shape each portion into flat, thin rectangles or squares.

2. Cook the Pantrucas:

    1. Heat the vegetable oil in a large skillet or frying pan over medium heat.

2. Carefully place the pantrucas in the hot oil and cook them for 2-3 minutes on each side, or until they are golden brown and cooked through.
3. Once cooked, remove the pantrucas from the skillet and set them aside.

3. Prepare the Soup:

1. In a large soup pot or Dutch oven, heat a drizzle of oil over medium heat.
2. Add the chopped onion, diced carrots, and diced celery to the pot. Cook for 5-7 minutes, or until the vegetables are softened.
3. Stir in the minced garlic, dried oregano, and dried thyme, and cook for another minute until fragrant.
4. Pour the chicken or beef broth into the pot and bring it to a simmer.
5. Season the soup with salt and pepper to taste.

4. Serve:

1. Once the soup is simmering, carefully add the cooked pantrucas to the pot.
2. Let the pantrucas simmer in the soup for a few minutes to absorb the flavors.
3. Ladle the soup and pantrucas into bowls and garnish with chopped fresh parsley, if desired.
4. Serve hot and enjoy this comforting Chilean dish!

Pantrucas are best enjoyed fresh and hot, and they make a satisfying meal on their own or served with crusty bread for dipping. Feel free to customize the soup with additional vegetables, herbs, or spices according to your taste preferences.

Sopa de Lentejas

Ingredientes:

- 1 taza de lentejas secas
- 6 tazas de caldo de verduras o agua
- 1 cebolla grande, picada
- 2 zanahorias, peladas y cortadas en cubitos
- 2 tallos de apio, cortados en rodajas
- 2 dientes de ajo, picados
- 1 tomate grande, cortado en cubitos
- 1 hoja de laurel
- 1 cucharadita de comino molido
- 1 cucharadita de pimentón
- 1/2 cucharadita de orégano seco
- Sal y pimienta al gusto
- Aceite de oliva para cocinar
- Perejil fresco picado para decorar (opcional)
- Jugo de limón para servir (opcional)

Instrucciones:

1. Preparar las Lentejas:
    - Enjuaga las lentejas bajo agua fría para quitar cualquier suciedad. Escúrrelas y revisa si hay piedrecillas u otros desechos.
    - En una olla grande, combina las lentejas y el caldo de verduras o agua. Lleva a ebullición y luego reduce el fuego a medio-bajo. Cocina las lentejas a fuego lento durante unos 20-25 minutos, o hasta que estén tiernas.
2. Preparar las Verduras:
    - Mientras las lentejas se cocinan, calienta un poco de aceite de oliva en una sartén grande a fuego medio.
    - Agrega la cebolla, las zanahorias y el apio, y saltea hasta que las verduras estén tiernas, unos 5-7 minutos.
    - Agrega el ajo picado y cocina por otros 2-3 minutos hasta que esté fragante.
    - Incorpora el tomate picado y cocina por unos minutos más hasta que se ablande.
3. Combinar Ingredientes:

- Agrega las verduras salteadas a la olla con las lentejas cocidas.
- Añade la hoja de laurel, el comino molido, el pimentón, el orégano seco, y sazona con sal y pimienta al gusto. Mezcla bien.
4. Dejar Reposar y Servir:
    - Deja que la sopa de lentejas repose a fuego lento durante unos minutos para que los sabores se mezclen.
    - Prueba y ajusta el condimento según sea necesario.
    - Sirve la sopa caliente, decorada con perejil fresco picado si lo deseas, y con un chorrito de jugo de limón en cada plato si prefieres un toque cítrico.
5. Disfrutar:
    - Sirve la sopa de lentejas como plato principal o acompáñala con pan crujiente para una comida reconfortante y deliciosa.

Esta receta es versátil, así que siéntete libre de ajustar las cantidades de ingredientes o agregar tus verduras favoritas para hacerla a tu gusto. ¡Espero que disfrutes de esta deliciosa sopa de lentejas al estilo chileno!